Marc Chagall
Ceramic Masterpieces

Marc Chagall
Ceramic Masterpieces

Edited by Roland Doschka

With contributions by

Roland Doschka

Hajo Düchting

Meret Meyer Graber

and Charles Sorlier

Prestel
Munich · Berlin · London · New York

This book was published on the occasion of the exhibition
of the same name held at the Stadthalle Balingen, Germany,
from 21 June–28 September 2003

Front cover: *Engaged Couple,* 1950 (see pp. 26–27)
Spine: *Woman with Flowers* (detail), 1962 (see pp. 172–173)
Frontispiece: *David and Bathsheba,* 1951 (see pp. 64–65)
Back cover: *The Two Birds,* 1961 (see pp. 162–163)

A catalogue record for this book is available from the British Library,
the Library of Congress and die Deutsche Bibliothek (http://dnb.ddb.de)

© Prestel Verlag, Munich · Berlin · London · New York 2003
© for works illustrated by Marc Chagall, by VG-Bild Kunst, Bonn, 2003

Photographic Credits: see p. 176
The Editor and Publisher would like to thank all individuals, institutions
and museums for kindly supplying pictorial material for publication

Prestel books are available worldwide. Please contact your nearest
bookseller or one of the following Prestel offices for information
concerning your local distributor:

Prestel Verlag
Königinstrasse 9, 80539 Munich
Tel. +49 (89) 38 17 09-0; Fax +49 (89) 38 17 09-35

Prestel Publishing Ltd.
4 Bloomsbury Place, London WC1A 2QA
Tel. +44 (020) 7323-5004; Fax +44 (020) 7636-8004

Prestel Publishing
175 Fifth Avenue, Suite 402, New York, NY 10010
Tel. +1 (212) 995-2720; Fax +1 (212) 995-2733

www.prestel.com

Translated from the German by John Gabriel, Worpswede
(Düchting/Meyer Graber) and Stephen Telfer, Edinburgh (Sorlier);
with thanks also to Alan Crump
Edited by Christopher Wynne
Designed and typeset by Saskia Helena Kruse, Munich
Cover design by Cilly Klotz
Originations by ReproLine, Munich
Printed by Aumüller KG, Regensburg
Bound by Conzella, Pfarrkirchen

Printed in Germany on acid-free paper
ISBN 3-7913-2941-3

Contents

For Meret Meyer Graber

The turbulent twentieth century is over: a century which saw not only fundamental political upheaval but also radical transformations in the art world. A not insignificant part of the latter is attributable to Marc Chagall whose artistic output spans nearly the whole of the century itself. Numerous exhibitions of his expansive œuvre demonstrate the extent of Chagall's contribution to twentieth-century art, the unique qualities of his iconographical paintings, which explore the very essence of his subject matter, and his use of mythical imagery.

Chagall is indeed to be placed among the great artists who paved the way for Modernism. The metaphors and symbols deeply embedded in Chagall's Russian homeland and the village life of his childhood, his intense feeling for colour, and the fundamental changes he made to pictorial space all render his painting distinctive in character and substantiate its uniqueness within the art of the twentieth century.

This volume, *Marc Chagall: Ceramic Masterpieces,* focuses on a relatively unknown aspect of the artist's œuvre – many people not being aware that Chagall was also a skilled ceramist. Around one hundred works, all of which are unique ceramic pieces produced by the artist in different workshops in the south of France, bear witness to his exceptional talent and craftsmanship.

The experience Chagall gained working independently with ceramics and enamel – while concentrating on form – was one of great chromatic intensity. The Apollonian bridled earth is cloaked in a Dionysian spectrum of colours, nuances and engobes. The form, plasticity, volume and tactile quality of the material all exerted a particularly strong fascination on Chagall.

It is, therefore, surely not surprising that it was precisely in the south of France that Chagall, in his search for new possibilities and forms of artistic expression, came across the material clay, since he had a kind of direct mystical perception of earth and light and both were sacred to him. His pictorial world seemed to have been made to be worked in this material. All the themes constituting the basis of his work are also found in his ceramic work: biblical scenes, mythical creatures, the circus, the Paris cycle, loving couples with flowers and finally Vence.

Chagall is arguably the greatest artist-craftsman of the twentieth century. Following the masterly skill shown in his expansive graphic output and the astonishingly successful implementation of his iconography in his magnificent stained glass windows, Chagall also proved his masterly skill in the use of engobe and enamel, terracotta and glaze.

Chagall revealed the secret of his creative genius in disarmingly simple words. He wrote: "Art is not created through theory – paintings and ceramics are created using one's hands and one's heart. Theories come later when the works themselves have already been completed. They originate from the works, they are not their origin."

Roland Doschka

Chagall and Ceramics
Hajo Düchting

Marc Chagall created a diverse and highly imaginative œuvre. His poetic paintings, dreamlike and shot through with symbolism, have contributed most to his great popularity. Chagall gave his dreamworld expression in nearly every visual medium, including gouache, watercolour, and the graphic techniques of etching and lithography. His activities also extended to designs for stage sets and costumes, such as for *Aleko, The Firebird* and *The Magic Flute.*

Less well-known are his ceramic works, despite the fact that he devoted a full decade of his career (1952–62) to untiring experiments in this medium. This may be due in part to the fragility of the one-off pieces which makes any exhibition a risky undertaking. Yet probably the main reason for their neglect has been the focus on Chagall's work in painting, by comparison to which the ceramics may well appear a negligible quantity.[1] Yet he produced a total of no less than 220 works in this medium, beginning with a small plate of 1949 and extending to his last, large-format ceramic wall piece, *Man and Bird,* of 1972.

Nor did the publication of a catalogue raisonné and a few exhibitions featuring Chagall's ceramics and sculptures change the situation much. The ceramic works presented in this volume will, we hope, encourage a deeper appreciation and involvement with this still largely unknown facet of Chagall's art.[2]

In October 1949, after returning to France from the United States and spending a period near Paris, Chagall settled in Saint-Jeannet, a small village in the hinterland of Nice, near the old Provençal town of Vence on the Mediterranean coast. Vence, like the surrounding towns Biot, Antibes and above all Vallauris, has an ancient ceramics tradition. In Vallauris, artists in the nineteenth century began to revive this old craft and infuse it with an avant-garde love of experiment. Clément Massier (1848–1917), for instance, founded a factory that introduced a special stoneware technique employing lustrous metallic glazes. In 1938, Suzanne and Georges Ramié established the famous 'Atelier du Plan' in Vallauris, which later became known under the name 'Madoura' and saw the creation of Picasso's renowned ceramic masterpieces. The revival of artistic ceramics is in fact principally due to Picasso whose innovations in the field were continually before Chagall's eyes.[3]

In the nineteenth century, Gauguin, too, turned to ceramics, in 1886 creating a few especially 'savage' pieces in the pottery shop of Chaplet and Delaherche. The Paris Autumn Salon of 1907 included ceramic works by Bonnard, Renoir, Redon, Derain, Rouault and Matisse. A fruitful collaboration developed between artists and potters, furthered by the efforts of Samuel Bing and Ambroise Vollard to infuse new life into the ancient craft by encouraging contemporary artists to try their hand at it. An example was the ceramicist André Metthey (1871–1920), who collaborated with the Fauves, especially Matisse and Derain. For Miró, in turn, the Catalonian potter Llorens Artigas proved important, helping the artist over crucial technical hurdles in the course of his work in this field.

After World War II, Aimé Maeght took up the idea of combining fine art with artisanry, an idea that had fallen on so fertile soil in the Bauhaus at Weimar and Dessau. In 1948 Maeght began exhibiting ceramics created by Miró in cooperation with Artigas in his Paris gallery. Chagall will have seen these pieces, since Maeght was his dealer in Europe from 1947 onwards. It was probably not least this creative, cosmopolitan milieu that encouraged Chagall to turn to new media such as printmaking and ceramics. In the preface to the catalogue of an exhibition at Curt Valentine's New York gallery in 1952, Chagall described this new experience in ceramics in his own words. Evoking the phenomonon of the transformation of earth into objects of art through the magic of fire, Chagall wrote:

"These few pieces, these few examples in ceramics, are a kind of appetizer: the result of my life in the south of France where the significance of this craft is still felt so strongly. Even the earth I stand on exudes light. She looks at me lovingly as if she wants to call me.

[1] As late as 1998, Monica Bohm-Duchen wrote in her book on Chagall: "In the ceramics, freely handled motifs, primarily of lovers or biblical figures, often borrowed directly from his paintings or prints, are superimposed on the clay without much adjustment to the very different nature of the medium." (*Chagall,* London, 1998, pp. 287–88)

[2] See the catalogue raisonné of the ceramics by Sylvie Forestier and Meret Meyer, *Chagall Keramik,* Munich, 1990. The most comprehensive review of Chagall's ceramics and sculptures to date was provided by the exhibition Hommage à Chagall, Grand Palais, Paris, 1969–70, which included 92 ceramic pieces. See also Sylvie Forestier, *Marc Chagall. Les années mediterranéenes 1949–1985* (exh. cat.), Musée National Message biblique Marc Chagall, Paris, 1994; and Camille Bourniquel, *Marc Chagall Ceramiques* (exh. cat.), Bouquinerie de l'Institut, Paris, 1999

[3] Picasso's need to be the first and best in every field did not stop short of ceramics and Chagall. Coming across a Chagall pot at the Madoura shop where Chagall intended to continue his work, Picasso 'completed' it by adding a floral ornament 'dans la manière de Chagall' (M. Bohm-Duchen, *Chagall,* p. 285)

I wanted to feel this earth just like the craftsmen of old and avoid any random ornamentation and, keeping within the limits of ceramics, I wanted to breathe the resonance of a simultaneously close yet distant art into it …"[4]

Chagall fabricated his first ceramic piece in 1949, at the 'Poterie des Remparts' in Antibes where he intially learned the basics of glazing by decorating Provençal kitchenware. Soon Chagall discovered the clay plaque as an autonomous pictorial field on which he could treat the themes of his paintings and graphic art in a new, more condensed, and therefore occasionally more highly expressive way. The small format of the plaque in no way inhibited Chagall. Sweeping lines, often emphasized by incising with knife or etching needle, were used to indicate the silhouettes of figures, animals or legendary creatures. In the subsequent kilning with lustrous metal glazes Chagall achieved quite innovative colouristic effects, ranging from a velvety surface to runs and textures reminiscent of watercolours (e.g. *Fox and Grapes*, 1950, pl. 13 and *The Flying Horse*, 1952, pl. 52). These pieces were followed by experiments with fire-brick clay. A mixture of raw and crushed or powdered fireclay lent the fired piece a grainy, porous consistency and increased the expressiveness of the colours (e.g. *Two Faces*, 1951, pl. 34 or *The Paris Opera*, 1953, pl. 61).

As in his graphic works, Chagall used to think from the outset in terms of cycles, such as the eleven plaques devoted to the fables of La Fontaine in 1950. When we compare these with the earlier etching sequence, we find an astonishingly sure grasp of the possibilities of the new painting support and its perfect exploitation for expressive purposes. The potentials of glazing are likewise masterfully explored, as in the contrast between matte and glossy passages which Chagall discovered and employed as an additional means of expression. In addition to the *Fables*, the artist began work in 1950 on a biblical cycle, just as subjects from the Bible began to play an ever greater role in his painting and printmaking at this period. No less than forty-one ceramics made between 1950 and 1952 were devoted to biblical themes which, thanks to the handy format of the plaques, entered the personal space and brought the message of the Bible directly into the private domain. Often these ceramic plaques were variations on subjects previously treated in paintings, gouaches or etchings, very skillfully adapted to the different conditions of the ceramic medium.

Chagall took advantage of the smaller format and special shapes, such as tondo and oval, to focus more closely on the essential elements of a visual narrative (e.g. *Joseph and Potiphar's Wife*, pl. 2). In other cases, lovingly rendered details served to supplement the message of a biblical story, as in the plaque *Abraham and the Three* Angels. Here Abraham, Sarah and the angels are accompanied by a camel at the edge of the plaque, a chicken and a donkey searching the ground for food immensely heighten the vitality of the composition.

Even in such monumental biblical themes as *Moses at the Spring* (pl. 22), Chagall managed to achieve a dramatic effect on the ceramic plaque quite comparable to that of the contemporaneous paintings. On the upright rectangle of the plaque, the figure arrangements previously established in drawings and gouaches take on a quite unprecedented concentration and accentuation. The horizontal format, in contrast, evidently encouraged a focus on the narrative element (e.g. *Judith and Holofernes,* pl. 18, *Joseph and Potiphar's Wife,* pl. 2, *David and Bathsheba,* pl. 28, *Noah's Ark, Descent from the Cross,* pl. 40). The way a story unfolds through time could find better expression on this format which, accordingly, suited the artist's love of storytelling and encouraged his inventiveness.

These gifts also came out in the legendary creatures and animals in which Chagall's creativity flourished in ceramics as much as it did in other media. The painted plate *Bird with Crown* (pl. 60) goes back to a Russian legend. It shows Sirine, the bird of paradise, a symbol of beauty and bliss in the world of Russian fairy-tales. Chagall had already depicted

[4] Sylvie Forestier and Meret Meyer, *Chagall Keramik,* p. 26

this bird on a monumental scale in 1945, on the curtain for a New York performance of Stravinsky's ballet, *The Firebird*. For the ceramic piece, Chagall chose a round format, the tondo, a traditional Italian Renaissance format on which the ornamental factor comes more strongly to the fore and the figure takes on an emblematic character.

Another major theme in Chagall's ceramics is the series of scenes from Paris, some unfolding in wide panorama-like depictions, others treated on a vertical format. For Chagall, Paris was the city of hope, of light and of the painting in which he developed his own inimitable style. In a cycle of oils, gouaches, lithographs and ceramics created between 1952 and 1954, the artist celebrated Paris, her monuments and squares, in visions of a dreamlike intensity. Dream and reality fuse in scenes such as that on the ceramic plate *The Paris Opera* (pl. 61), where, against a background in delicate shades of pink, a ballerina floats high above the building, flanked at the right edge by an oversized bouquet of roses.

Paris also appears on one of the earliest wall ceramics, *Pont-Neuf* (1950–52). Here the bridge and the Seine landscape merely form the background for a pair of lovers floating in the air – one of Chagall's best known motifs – which appears again and again in his work in ceramics as in other media.

Wall-mounted pieces, to which he began to devote himself in 1950, confronted Chagall with quite new problems, as regards both dimensions and integration of the picture into the architectural setting. At the outset, he created simple pieces consisting of four tiles *(The Cock,* pl. 6). As his sureness of handling increased, Chagall advanced to ever more complex wall pieces, such as the twelve-plaque composition *The Clock* (1950–52, pl. 44), in which time stands still for the lovers encased in a clock against a night-blue background. This time, it is not Paris that provides the setting but tiny wooden houses huddled at the lower right, an evocation drawn from Chagall's storehouse of memories from his Russian home village, Vitebsk.

The larger area of the wall tiles invited a reduction and monumentalization of motif, as seen in *The Cock* (see above), whose talons in fact extend across the decorative border. The bird, rendered in sparing graphic strokes, stands out effectively from the yellow slip of the background, while in the interior of the motif, lovers rendered in red yearningly approach each other.

More ambitious than such intimate depictions is the cycle of the *Message Biblique* which Chagall also addressed in the medium of wall-mounted ceramics. For the chapel Notre-Dame de Toutes Grâces in Assy (Savoy), he designed a wall piece on the subject of *The Journey Through the Red Sea* (pl. 39), which was executed in 1956 on ninety tiles. In 1959, Chagall addressed himself to the project of translating *The Creation of Mankind* (pl. 87, 88) into a wall-mounted ceramic. The six finished pieces form a sequence in which the motif is sub-jected to ever-new variations. Here Chagall once again shows himself to be a master of col-oration who, in ceramic glazes as much as oils, was capable of producing intense colour con-trasts and values, in which blue, one of his principal colours, plays a key role in accentuat-ing the pictorial motif. The rough texture of the fireclay lends the series an additional drama.

Already in the plaques, Chagall had become familiar with and exploited all the potentials of the ceramic medium. All that was lacking was the third dimension, without which the true essence of ceramics could not be captured. The final chapter of Chagall's work in the field was thus devoted to sculpted vases and ceramic sculptures. The vase shape was especially suited to depictions of nudes, and its swelling forms lent these a more clearly sexual con-notation than in paintings (e.g. *David and Bathsheba in the Light of the Moon,* pl. 57, and *A Summer Night's Dream,* pl. 46).

In developing the vases, Chagall took the exaggeration and stylization of forms to the point of complex plastic configurations that were completely divorced from the natural model. Beginning with basic plastic forms, he kneaded and shaped the clay into ever more fantastic configurations which transcended the limited field of utilitarian ceramics and entered that of

Vence, 1954. From left to right: *The Chimera,* 1954, p. 133, *Two People,* 1954, *The Peasant at the Well,* 1952, *The Cock, The Cock,* 1954, pp. 134–35

Marc Chagall in the Atelier Madoura, Vallauris, 1962

free sculpture. There emerged 'sculpted vases' (*Sculpted Vase,* pl. 54) which, though still clearly exhibiting the fundamental vase shape, subjected it to a metamorphosis by means of distortions and superimpositions.

The vase *Woman with Flowers* (pl. 96) exhibits the voluptuous shapes of a female nude, yet simultaneously employs the same configuration to evoke a rearing donkey. Here Chagall exploits to the full the sensuous traits of the ceramic vase and links its tactile qualities with the theme of the loving couple, which here becomes veritably 'graspable'.

Another sculpted vase takes up the undulating silhouette of a female head and employs it as the back wall of a vase open to the front whose lower edge is adorned by a yellow donkey. Such configurations were subsequently taken to the point of zoomorphic mergers of the basic vase shape with animal depictions, as in the famous *Cock* (pl. 72), a chimera covered with a light-coloured enamel glaze whose resemblance to a cock is truly distant. The body of the undefinable creature expands into a great vessel standing on two plump paws. The head, with vessel's opening, consists merely of a single great bird's bill. Inscribed on the belly of the 'vase' are a pair of lovers and a reclining female nude. Perhaps these motifs refer to the meaning of the vase-sculpture, an embodiment of the power of love, of which the cock is the sexual symbol. In other ceramic pieces by Chagall the vase function has been abandoned entirely, resulting in works of an autonomy perhaps comparable only to Miró's ceramic creations.

The Lovers and the Beast (pl. 79) is a good example of this creative, self-perpetuating dynamism which spells out the artist's repertoire of motifs like a visual alphabet. The lower part of the round, hollow vessel is formed by an embracing couple whose heads merge into a double face. Above this, an applied animal shape appears – a donkey whose tail forms a sort of handle. Set in the beast's back are two apertures that may indicate the vessel's function. Similar biomorphic mergers of vase shape with objective motif often appear in the culminating phase of Chagall's work in ceramics, as, for example, in the pieces *Large Figures* (pl. 93), *Second Vase-Woman,* or in the humorous vase *The Blue Donkey* (pl. 73), whose handles are made from the donkey's forefeet. Such features reflect the artist's enjoyment of transcending the narrow limits of this old craft, and making artistic incursions that lend it entirely new dimensions.

Although Chagall's work in ceramics was limited in time, it holds a very special place within his œuvre as a whole. Its variety of forms and themes, its Baroque enjoyment of metamorphosis, and the love of experiment reflected in the use of glazes and surface effects attests to the artist's unflagging vitality and creative powers. In addition to their thematic richness, Chagall's ceramics are also objects of aesthetic pleasure, whose richly textured surfaces appeal in ever-new ways not only to the eye but to the caressing hand.

Gaston Bachelard, in his preface to the catalogue of the second exhibition of Chagall's ceramics at Galerie Maeght in 1952, poetically described this miraculous marriage of earth and fire: "How wonderful is an age like ours, when the greatest painters wish to become potters and ceramicists! They bring colours to a boil. Through fire, they create light. They discover chemistry with their eyes; they would have matter react in a way that is pleasing to the eye. Out of the soft, dull, lustreless mass they foresee luminous enamel."[5]

5   Quoted in ibid., p. 9

Chagall's Reverence for Soil

Meret Meyer Graber

Marc Chagall's long-awaited return to France (*"Paris, you are my second Vitebsk"*[1]) from his period of exile in America in 1948–49 had a profound effect on his art. With the exception of works produced in Cranberry Lake, NY, Chagall painted no other landscape in the United States. Orgeval, near Saint-Germain-en-Laye, is where he settled on his return. The landscapes, towns and villages Chagall travelled through had preoccupied him from 1923 until his forced emigration to the United States in 1940. The works he produced later were generally inspired by the Mediterranean region, particularly after he settled in Vence in 1949–50.

During this period his compositions began to take on a breadth which engulfed the entire picture plane. His palette was comparatively restricted, in both the monochrome/bichrome ink drawings and the works on canvas. The Côte d'Azur bathed in blue or suffused with the brilliant light of the South of France had always fascinated the artist from as early as the 1920s.

At last he was able to give his imagination free rein and revel in the happiness of returning to what he referred to as his 'second home'. The formats grew to monumental proportions and Chagall's curiosity about various artistic techniques was once again reawakened and intensified. Ceramics permitted the artist to work directly with the clay of Provence, the very soil from which his new French citizenship and identity had grown since 1937. The physical contact with the earth in the form of clay enhanced the meaning of this experience and created the foundation of security and 'home'.

On the Côte d'Azur, the ceramic medium was veritably so strong a presence that Chagall felt drawn to it, since there were also a series of workshops which had had a long history of collaboration with major modernist artists. Chagall's first ceramics emerged in 1949, at the atelier of Madame Bonnaud in Antibes, followed in 1950 by pieces done at the Poterie des Remparts (e.g. the *Fables* plates), with the ceramic expert Serge Ramel in Vence, at the Atelier de l'Hospied in Golfe-Juan. From 1951 to 1962, Chagall's ceramics were created solely at Madoura, in the atelier of Serge and Suzanne Ramié in Vallauris, where Picasso also worked.

For his first ceramics the artist painted motifs on existing Provençal ware. All the *Fables* motifs were produced on rectangular plates, which corresponded to the format of his paintings (during the 1920s Chagall had already executed *Fables* cycles in gouache on paper and as etchings). His use of kitchenware as a painting ground was an ideal conduit for Chagall to integrate himself into the Provençal life of ancient France and to be given the opportunity to expand artistically and abundantly on locally produced ceramics.

The white Provençal ware created for his daughter's wedding celebration in Madoura in 1951 comprises some seventy-five individual pieces – cups, plates, bowls, platters and a soup tureen – with fantastic and poetic images. The pieces exude happiness and convey Chagall's blessings in blue or bluish-brown brush drawings. Each piece was decorated differently – with flowers, still lifes, loving couples, nudes, animals and circus motifs.

The glossy white ground of the honest, unpretentious ceramic ware, integrated into the composition, is used to exploit negative spaces that enhance the colours (see also the individual tile, *Les fiancés,* 1950, pl. 1). In the last mural ceramics (e.g. *Greek Landscape,* 1962, pl. 91), the white light reflected by the unpainted surface (which in the mural pieces of the intervening years had been completely painted) becomes part of the 'picture' coupled within the now increasingly painterly compositions.

Chagall began to explore possibilities for reinforcing the background concept as an integral part of his compositions. On the usually monochromatic backgrounds of the *Fable* plates (from white and beige to brown and blue) the stories emerge from techniques which range

Marc Chagall working on a ceramic plate at Madoura, Vallauris, *c.* 1955

[1] Marc Chagall, *My Life,* New York 1960, p. 116

14

from incised line to relief colour, matte surfaces alternating with gloss, resulting in a combination of fascinating textures of great variety and richness.

As if following a quick musical rhythm, the artist pressed thumb and fingers into various areas of the forms, blurring the smoothness of the clay, gently but firmly modelling it as if in anticipation of the surprises revealed through a piece's magical reincarnation in the kiln and the very process of transformation.

In 1952–53, Chagall used ever more expansive and alternative forms coupled with paint to express ever greater freedom. Cycles of ceramics emerged, such as the Paris series on plates (*The Paris Opera,* pl. 61, 62, *The Bastille,* pl. 63, *In Front of Notre-Dame,* 1953, pl. 65) and biblical subjects on platters, vases, vessels and mural ceramics. The uneven surfaces, some created by the technique of granulated fireclay affording a far more physical or tactile character. The works become quasi-landscapes in which real or imagined scenes are enacted. The depicted representation evolves from the 'picture' adopting its own internal dynamism.

Chagall began to redefine form by newly-found creative inventions and interventions, usually retaining the object's original function but adding a small number of sculptural appendages. The longer the artist immersed himself in the art of ceramics, the more he divorced himself from original generic shapes. In doing so it allowed for more dominant sculptural elements to supercede (e.g. the vases *The House,* 1952, pl. 45; *Sculpted Vase,* 1952, pl. 54; *Peasant at the Well,* 1952–53, pl. 58, 59; *The Cock,* 1954, pl. 72; *The Chimera,* 1954, pl. 71; *The Lovers and the Beast,* 1957, pl. 79; *The Stroll,* 1961, pl. 89; and the plate *The Two Birds,* 1961, pl. 90). The three-dimensional ceramic pieces with additional painted figures in low relief engender a dialogue between the interior form and all aspects of their exterior. An essential feature is the way the clay 'skin' of these figures appears to breathe; partly matte and silky and partly glossy with engraved furrows. They are simultaneously both strong and fragile. The pieces alternately absorb and reflect light with a brilliance that emanates from a unique eternal energy. Bachelard's "With fire they create light" convincingly demonstrates the intensity of much of Chagall's ceramic work[2].

After thirteen years of involvement with ceramics, the artist felt that he had exhausted the potential of this medium. As he embarked on a search for intriguing surprises and artis-

2 Gaston Bachelard, 'La lumière des origines', in *Chagall Monumental,* Paris 1973, p. 130

La Colline, Vence, *c.* 1955

Marc Chagall working on a design for the mosaic
The Cock (a work intended for Ravenna but never
realized), Vence, *c.* 1957

tic innovations, in 1962 his interest in ceramics waned and, in parallel with his painting, he turned to other manifestations drawn from the ground: stone for sculpture and glass from sand.

During the years Chagall worked with ceramics, he did not relegate painting and drawing to a subordinate position. On the contrary, painting and ceramics (like all of the media he focused on) remained in continuous dialogue, the one enriching the other in a mutual fusion. Experience with ceramics, working with the clay of the earth, flowed into his painting and led to a redefinition and restructuring of the painted surface. This was and always remained the foremost concern of the painter Marc Chagall.

Ceramics and Sculptures

Charles Sorlier

Ceramics occupy a significant place in Chagall's artistic output even if they are relatively unknown. His pieces have been exhibited rarely and only partially. They include vases and vessels in innovative shapes that were mostly the property of the artist who seldom wished to part company with them because of their fragile nature.

Chagall was without question one of the twentieth century's greatest artist-craftsman (in antiquity, one expression was used to encompass both activities) and he employed the same skills in both disciplines. Chagall's graphic output amounts to almost five hundred copper-plate prints and woodcuts, including the bibliophile masterpieces commissioned by Ambroise Vollard *The Dead Souls* (1924–25), *La Fontaine's Fables* (1926–31) and *The Bible* (1931–56). Chagall produced 1000 lithographs in black and white and colour, some of which marked the very pinnacle of colour lithography, among them *Daphnis and Chloé* (1957–61), *Exodus* (1964–66) and *The Circus* (1962–67).

Chagall produced around fifty stained-glass windows. His tapestries (seven in all, including three in the Knesset in Jerusalem) and mosaics (seven walls including the large piece at the Faculty of Science of the University of Nice inspired by the myth of Odysseus) account for a relatively small percentage of his overall artistic output. This can be explained quite simply: Chagall, the ingenious artist-craftsman largely had to depend on weavers and mosaicists to execute such work for him; he himself, however, preferred working in solitude and it is obvious that no one could take his place.

By contrast, lithography and etching posed no difficulties – the painter being alone with his stone or copperplate. The printer became involved only at the point of printing under the

Marc Chagall in Vence, April 1951

guidance of the artist who continued to make corrections until he was completely happy with the result.

When it came to stained glass windows, Charles Marq placed his vast technical expertise in the service of the artist and withdrew behind the figure of his 'client'. Artist and glassmaker had lengthy discussions about the choice of glass, its colouring and lead mounts. And when the structure for a stained-glass window had finally been decided upon, it was Chagall alone who day by day created the essence of the work, its innermost spirit, its design, in an attempt to achieve – if not complete satisfaction (for like every artist, Chagall had doubts about his work) – at least "a modest result that can hold its own alongside a bouquet of flowers." Sculpture and ceramics are in complete harmony with the artist's will. There is no intermediary between the artist's hands and his material, and Chagall, unlike most artists, was not content with decorating pieces made by professional potters. He himself moulded his clay and created original forms, thus becoming – unusually – a painter sculpting in ceramic. Chagall's profound originality is here expressed in his material. His imagination and poetic vision flowed freely and he was not restricted by any previously drawn drafts. His fantasies were given their ultimate form of expression. The sensuousness of the *Golden Age* matches the humour of the *Cockerel* with its *Ubu Roi*-like attributions. Vitebsk is re-created in *Peasant at the Well,* pl. 58, 59, or the *Lovers with Animal.* The arbitrary form of *Bowl with Sculpture* is transformed into three-dimensional reality. Chagall first created ceramic pieces in 1950 in various workshops: at Mme Bonneau's in Antibes, Serge Ramel's ceramics workshops in Vence and Antibes, and in the pottery 'L'Hospied' in Golfe-Juan. Most of the pieces featured in this volume, however, were realised in Georges and Suzanne Ramié's Atelier Madoura in Vallauris.

Some of Chagall's works were exhibited in Paris in 1950 and 1957, in New York in 1952, in Turin in 1963, in Basel and Berne in 1956, in Cannes in 1962 and finally, from December 1969 to March 1970, in the Grand Palais in Paris (*Hommage à Chagall*) – the only exhibition to introduce the public to the artist's complete œuvre of sculptures and ceramics (the exhibition catalogue listed ninety-two ceramics and twenty-six sculptures).

Gaston Bachelard described these first successful shows as follows: "How wonderful this era of ours is: the greatest painters are happy to work as ceramicists and potters. In this way they can fire their colours and with flames they create light. Marc Chagall immediately became a master of this satanic form of painting that leaves the two-dimensional plane and penetrates the depths of chemistry."

"Ceramics," according to Chagall, "is the combination of earth and fire, nothing else. If you give the fire something good, it will return a little of it to you, but if it is bad, everything shatters, and nothing remains. Nothing can be done about it; fire is pitiless in its judgement."

Fortunately for us, fire treated Chagall's work mercifully. Besides his talent, he put his heart into it. Perhaps he did so with a saying of Mozart's at the back of his mind, one he was so fond of quoting: "Talent and genius are nothing; a work of art can be nothing but love, love, love."

Marc Chagall working on the vase *Large Figures*, 1962, p. 168, Madoura, Vallauris

Art is not created through Theory
Roland Doschka

It comes as no real surprise that, in the first half of the twentieth century in France, a multitude of ceramic works and faïence of high artistic value can be found. At around the turn of that century, none other than Matisse, Rouault and Vlaminck ventured into the demanding field of ceramics and left proven evidence of their skill. They were soon followed by Dufy, Léger, Braque, Chagall, Cocteau, and Miró, as well as by Picasso, who set his own artistic accents.

The diversity of any artistic expression which stretches to include ceramics requires an artist to be a true 'all rounder', although being skilled in many areas of art and in many techniques is something that cannot be taken for granted.

In the past, however, it could. From Antiquity right through until the late Renaissance period, universality was a common phenomenon. Most artists were both sculptors and painters and occasionally even architects. Art and science were often united in one and the same person. But since the seventeenth century, a painter has remained a painter and a sculptor, a sculptor. There are few exceptions to this rule.

We have to jump as far as the nineteenth century before we come across a couple of painters again who are also sculptors. Think of Daumier, Degas, Renoir and Gauguin. However, it is equally interesting to note that the Impressionists Monet, Pissarro and Sisley never ventured onto the realm of sculpture, neither did Cézanne or van Gogh. The play of light and its study fascinated them, not the tangible side. Only the Fauves and the Cubists were at ease in both media. Matisse, Derain, Braque, Gris and Léger were both skilful painters and sculptors. It is, however, especially clear in the case of Picasso that painting, graphic art and sculpture are on the same plane.

Whenever these artists focussed their attention on ceramics, they had to rely on the advice and help of the ceramists already acknowledged as masters in working with clay and glazes.

André Metthey, who was born in 1871 in Laignes (Côte d'Or) and died in Asnières, near Paris in 1920, was already famous on account of a number of exhibitions of his own ceramic work. Specialist magazines and critics were already showing a keen interest in his work when it came to a fruitful cooperation between Metthey and the Fauve painters.

Hans-Jürgen Heuser says in his essay 'French Ceramics between 1850 and 1910': "In 1903 Metthey moved to Asnières, a suburb of Paris on the banks of the Seine. As he done earlier, he continued to produce stoneware but soon ventured into making faïence. In 1905 there were reports of him working with so-called *pâtes rapportées,* which can only be applied to stoneware or porcelain, and of painting, which would suggest faïence. That he was working in this medium seems to be confirmed by Ambroise Vollard who learnt about his faïence work at that time. He had suggested working together with those Fauves painters he represented, namely Bonnard, Denis, Derain, Puy, Matisse, Laprade, Maillol, K.X. Roussel, Rouault, Valtat and Vlaminck. In 1907 the result was exhibited in the Salon d'Automne." A further name should be mentioned at this point. After World War I, the Catalan ceramist Llorens Artigas moved to Paris where he worked with Dufy, Miró and Braque. However, here it was the ceramist who sought advice from the painter to work the surface. Again it was not the painter himself who wished to express his artistic idea through ceramics, through close contact with the material, with the elements earth, water, air and fire.

It was Pablo Picasso who, with the passion and thoroughness of a genius, really started to work with clay. But he could not do without the help and advice of Georges and Suzanne Ramié who gave him advice and encouraged him in the early stages of his working with ceramics. The same is true for the cooperation between Georges and Suzanne Ramié on the one hand and Chagall. Similarly, Cocteau's ceramic works, which came into being in the wake of Picasso's work, would not have been realized without the help of Marie-Madeline Jolly and Philippe Madeline.

Ceramics show us the artists' versatility on the one hand and, on the other, the positive cooperation with others who can appreciate the magnificence of a successful work of art and be absorbed by it. Since little has been published about Chagall's ceramic œuvre, I would like to take a closer look at these unique works.

It is surely not surprising that it was precisely in the south of France that Chagall, in his search for new possibilities and forms of artistic expression, came across the material clay, since he had a kind of direct mystical perception of earth and light and both were sacred to him. He combined the solidity of matter with the transparency and intangibility of light that penetrates everything. Full of enthusiasm Chagall said: "Even the earth I stand on exudes light. She looks at me lovingly as if she wants to call me." And he answers this call, shortens the distance and draws near: "I wanted to feel this earth just like the craftsmen of old and, keeping within the limits of ceramics, I wanted to breathe the resonance of a simultaneously close yet distant art into it."

To do so the colourist was initially interested in increasing the number of colours in his palette, in adding different shades of colour and in the special effect they had on clay. What he so skilfully mastered in painting is equally present in his ceramics. The colours are captivating; fabulously intoxicating colours rid material of their gravity, render objects immaterial, letting them drift away with buoyant lightness.

The Apollonian bridled earth is covered with a Dionysian spectrum of colours, nuances and shades. Ceramics is, however, not solely a splendidly coloured iconography. The shape, the plasticity, the move into the spacial, into the third dimension, is equally a part of it. In the originally smooth and flat surface of his first works – in which pre-shaped plates were painted, followed by large-format wall ceramics which reached their artistic zenith in the baptistery of the church on the Plateau d'Assy – Chagall added movement and subtle rhythm to his work by creating depth and curves, sometimes filigree, sometimes drawn out plastically. The ceramic work *Couple* is a very striking example of this. It shows that Chagall was not

Picasso and Chagall in the Atelier Madoura,

Vallauris, early 1950s

Marc Chagall in his studio in La Colline,
Saint Paul de Vence, c. 1970

satisfied with painting the clay only, but had to model it himself, working at its surface. It was only a small step toward sculpting which Chagall ultimately reaches through ceramics. The most important experience that Chagall made as a result of working with ceramics was not primarily his discovery of the third dimension in art but rather the primal experience of the simple act of creation. The artist can prepare the work; he can let it take form spiritually and emotionally, but it can only be completed by fire. It is fire that brings about the greatest symbiosis, the unity of material and colour. Both only acquire their ultimate form and permanent character when fired and through the firing. Through fire, the primal forces of an erupting lava flow, slowly cooling and taking on a new shape – an initially creative and purely natural act – is thus imitated and completed. Something of the basic, primeval *élan vital* in the sense used by the philosopher Henri Bergson, rises through the flames, burns light and breathes life into the ceramic piece. That is where we find the archetypal secret of the transformation from appearance into being. The image and its colour are fused into the material to form an inseparable entity, much the same as the two levels of a 'linguistic sign'.

Not only the artist is involved in the genesis of a work of art but – and this question arises time and again – what will the fire will create from the shapes and colours in an orgy of consumption and transformation? Chagall was well aware of that and confessed: "Sometimes the fire releases the products of my pains with respect from the kiln, but other times they emerge as grotesque and ridiculous shapes. The old elements remind me all too well that my means are limited."

It would certainly be wrong to consider Chagall's ceramic work merely as an interesting supplement to his œuvre. As always, he worked with utter passion and the conviction of his creative personality, impassioned by the message he so wanted to voice. I realize that ceramics won his direct and very special devotion. It was only for some fifteen years, from 1950 onwards, that Chagall worked actively in this medium but his testimony to this period can still be admired, as a loyal companion, in La Colline in Saint Paul de Vence. All the themes constituting the basis of his work are also found in his ceramic work: biblical scenes, mythical creatures, the circus, the Paris cycle, loving couples with flowers and finally Vence. Many times Chagall made extremely accurate sketches before giving his ceramic work its definite form.

What Chagall undertook in this fascinating medium was more than just a sporadic experiment. Otherwise, how he achieved such a level of mastery in his working of engobe, enamel, glazes and terracotta would barely be comprehensible. On top of this comes the inexplicable and unrepeatable secret of every creation. Chagall expressed this aptly: "Art is not created through theory – paintings and ceramics are created using one's hands and heart. Theories come later when the works themselves have already been completed. They originate from the works, they are not their origin."

PLATES

1 Engaged Couple (*Les fiancés*)

1950, tile, 15.7 x 15.4 cm

Coloured clay, decorated using oxides on white enamel,

glazed, signed bottom left 'Chagall',

with dedication, signed and dated on reverse

'Pour Ida – Papa Vence 1950'

Private collection

2 Joseph and Potiphar's Wife

(*Joseph et la femme de Putiphar*)

1950, platter, 28.8 x 35.4 cm

Moulded, coloured clay, decoration with engobe

and oxides, incised with knife and etching needle,

glazed, signed and dated 'Marc Chagall Antibes 1950'

Private collection

3 Double Face in Green
(*Double visage en vert*)
1950, plate, diameter 23.5 cm
Moulded, white clay, decorated using oxides,
incised with knife and etching needle, glazed,
signature incised at bottom 'Chagall'
Private collection

4 Lovers with Goats

(*Amoureux avec chèvre*)

1950, platter, 26.5 x 23 cm

Moulded, decoration with engobe and oxides

on black engobe, signed and dated on reverse

Private collection

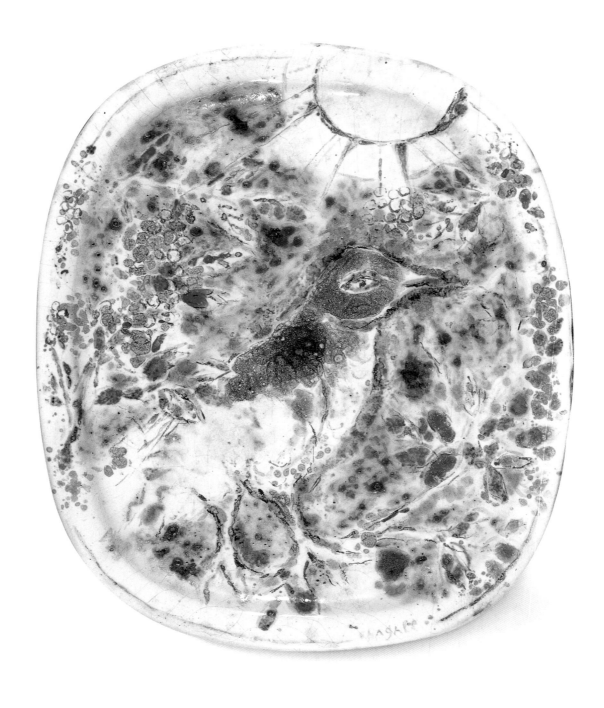

5 Flowers and Bird

(*Fleurs et oiseau*)

1950, platter, 27 x 23 cm

Moulded and modelled, brown clay,

decorated using oxides on white enamel,

signed and dated on reverse 'Chagall 1950'

Private collection

6 The Cock

(*Le coq*)

1950, wall ceramic (4 tiles), 25 x 27.2 cm

White clay, decorated using oxides, glazed,

signed bottom left 'Chagall'

Private collection, courtesy Yves Lebouc

7 The Two Doves

(*Les deux pigeons*)

1950, platter, 20 x 17 cm

Moulded, coloured clay, decoration with engobe

on oxides, incised with knife and etching needle,

glazed, signature incised at bottom left 'Chagall'

Private collection

8 The Cat that Changed into a Woman
(*La chatte métamorphosée en femme*)
1950, platter, 22.5 x 19.5 cm
Moulded, decorated using oxides on engobe,
incised with knife and etching needle, glazed,
signature incised at bottom right 'Chagall'
Private collection

9 The Raven and the Fox

(*Le corbeau et le renard*)

1950, platter, 22.5 x 19.8 cm

Moulded, coloured clay, painted using oxides

on white enamel, signed at bottom right 'Chagall'

Private collection

10 The Wolf and the Lamb

(*Le loup et l'agneau*)

1950, platter, 19.5 x 22.5 cm

Moulded, brown clay, decorated using oxides

on engobe, incised with knife and etching needle,

signature incised at bottom left 'Chagall'

Private collection

11 The Fox and the Stork

(*Le renard et la cigogne*)

1950, platter, 22.5 x 19.5 cm

Moulded, coloured clay, decoration with engobe

and oxides on enamel, incised with knife and

etching needle, glazed, signature 'Chagall'

Private collection

12 The Dog with its Master's Dinner
around its Neck
(*Le chien qui porte à son cou le dîner
de son maître*)
1950, platter, 19.5 x 22.5 cm
Moulded, doloured clay, decoration with engobe
and oxides, incised with knife and etching needle,
signature incised at bottom right 'Chagall'
Private collection

13 Fox and Grapes
(*Le renard et les raisins*)
1950, platter, 22.5 x 19.5 cm
Moulded, coloured clay, decoration with engobe
and oxides on enamel, incised with knife and
etching needle, signature incised at bottom right
'Chagall'
Private collection

14 Two Bulls and a Fox
(*Les deux taureaux et une grenouille*)
1950, platter, 19.5 x 22.5 cm
Moulded, coloured clay, decorated using oxides
on engobe, incised with knife and etching needle,
signed at bottom 'Chagall'
Private collection

15 The Green Goat

(*La chèvre verte*)

1950, platter, 28.5 x 33 cm

Turned and modelled, coloured clay, decorated

using oxides, incised with knife and etching needle,

glazed, signed at bottom 'Chagall'

Private collection

16 The Donkey (*L'âne*)

1950, platter, 26 x 20 cm

Moulded, coloured clay, decorated using oxides,

incised with knife and etching needle,

signed at bottom right 'Chagall', signed and

dated on reverse 'Chagall Antibe 1950'

Private collection

17 The Visiting Donkey
(*L'âne en visite*)
1950, platter, 16 x 18.7 cm
Moulded, coloured clay, decoration with engobe
and oxides, incised with knife and etching needle,
signature incised at top 'Chagall'
Private collection

18 Judith and Holofernes

(*Judith et Holopherne*)

1950, platter, 22.5 x 27 cm

Moulded and modelled, decoration with engobe

and oxides on white enamel, signed at bottom right

'Chagall' and on reverse 'Chagall', Antibes

Private collection

19 Samson Tears down the Pillars
in the Temple
(*Samson brisant les colonnes du temple*)

1950, platter, 32.5 x 28 cm

Moulded, decoration with engobe and oxides on

white enamel, signed at bottom 'Chagall',

signed and dated on reverse 'Chagall, Antibes 1950'

Private collection

20 Jacob's Blessing (*La bénédiction*)

1950, platter, 29 x 23.5 cm

Moulded, white clay, decoration with engobe and oxides,

incised with knife and etching needle,

signature incised at bottom right 'Chagall'

Private collection

21 Jacob's Ladder
(*L'échelle de Jacob*)
1950, platter, 28.7 x 23.3 cm
Moulded, coloured clay, decorated using oxides
on white enamel, glazed, signed bottom left 'Chagall'
Private collection

22 Moses at the Spring

(*Moïse à la source*)

1950, platter, 45 x 36 cm

Moulded and modelled, coloured clay,

decoration with engobe and oxides,

incised with knife and etching needle,

glazed, signed at bottom 'Chagall',

signed and dated on reverse 'Chagall 1950'

Private collection

23 Jacob's Dream
(*Le songe de Jacob*)
1950, platter, 33.2 x 43 cm
Moulded and modelled, coloured clay,
decoration with engobe and oxides,
incised with knife and etching needle,
glazed, signed at bottom 'Chagall',
signed and dated on reverse 'Chagall 1950'
Private collection

24 Moses and the Ten Commandments
(*Moïse et les Tables de la Loi*)
1950, platter, 30.8 x 25.2 cm
Moulded and modelled, white clay,
decoration with engobe and oxides,
incised with knife and etching needle,
glazed, signed at bottom right 'Chagall'
Private collection

25 David with the Lyre

(*David à la lyre*)

1950, platter, 27.5 x 22.5 cm

Moulded, coloured clay, decoration with engobe

and oxides, incised with knife and etching needle,

glazed, signed and dated 'Marc Chagall Antibes 1950'

Private collection

26 David and Saul

(*David et Saül*)

1950, platter, 34.5 x 31 cm

Moulded and modelled, decoration with engobe

and oxides, incised with knife and etching needle,

glazed, signed at bottom right 'Chagall',

signed and dated on reverse

'Marc Chagall Antibes 1950'

Private collection

27 Christ on the Cross

(*Le Christ en croix*)

1950, platter, 27 x 22.8 cm

Moulded and modelled, white clay,

decoration with engobe and oxides on white enamel,

signed at bottom right 'Chagall',

signed and dated on reverse 'Chagall 1950'

Private collection

28 David and Bathsheba

(*David et Bethsabée*)

1951, picture platter, 32 x 27 cm

Fire-brick clay, decoration with engobe and oxides,

partly with enamel applied by brush,

signed at bottom right 'Chagall'

Private collection

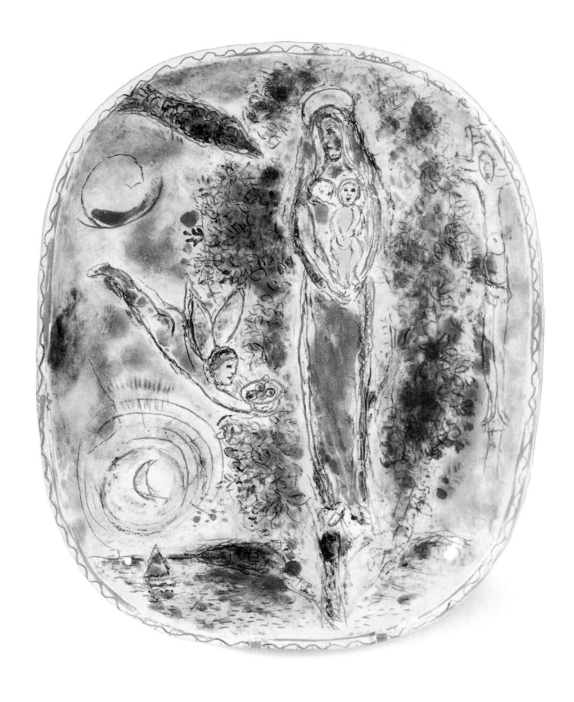

29 The Virgin as a Tree

(*La Madone à l'arbre*)

1951, platter, 41 x 33 cm

Moulded, brown Clay, decoration with engobe

and oxides, incised with knife and etching needle,

glazed, signed and dated on reverse

'Marc Chagall Vence 1951'

Private collection, courtesy Daniel Malingue, Paris

30 Still Life with Fruit

(*Nature mort aux fruits*)

1951, platter, diameter 30.5 cm

Turned and modelled, white clay decoration with

engobe and oxides, incised with knife and

etching needle, glazed, signed at bottom right 'Chagall',

signed and dated on reverse 'Chagall 1951'

Private collection

31 The Milkmaid and the Jug of Milk

(*La laitière et le pot au lait*)

1951, platter, 22.7 x 19.8 cm

Moulded, coloured clay, decoration with engobe and

oxides and enamel, incised with knife and etching needle,

glazed, incised signature at bottom 'Chagall'

Private collection

32 Flowers (*Fleurs*)

1951, picture platter, 31.8 x 26.8 cm

Fire-brick clay, decoration with engobe and oxides,

partly with enamel applied by brush,

signed at bottom right 'Chagall',

with dedication, signed and dated on reverse

'Pour Ida Bonne Année 1952 Papa Chagall'

Private collection

33 Double Profile of David and Bathsheba
(*David et Bethsabée au double profil*)
1951, platter, 42 x 35 cm
Moulded, white clay, decoration with engobe
and oxides, incised with knife and etching needle,
partly with enamel applied by brush,
signed at bottom right 'Chagall'
Private collection

34 Two Faces (*Les deux visages*)

1951, platter, 38 x 24 cm

Moulded and modelled, fire-brick clay,

decoration with engobe and oxides,

incised with knife and etching needle, glazed,

signed on reverse 'Chagall 1951'

Private collection

35 Mother and Child

(*La mère et l'enfant*)

1951, platter, diameter 37 cm

Moulded, brown clay, decorated using oxides on

black engobe, incised with knife, partly with enamel

applied by brush, signed on reverse 'Chagall'

Private collection

36 Embracing Lovers

(*Amoureux enlacés*)

1951, platter, 41.5 x 31.5 cm

Moulded and modelled, decoration with engobe

and oxides, incised with knife and etching needle,

glazed, signed at bottom right 'Chagall',

signed and dated on reverse 'Chagall 1951 Vence'

Private collection

37 Lover with Bird

(*Amoureux à l'oiseau*)

1951, platter, 28.5 x 22.5 cm

Moulded, decorated using oxides on engobe,

glazed, signed at bottom right 'Chagall',

signed and dated on reverse

Private collection

38 Woman and Bird

(*Femme sur oiseau*)

1951, picture platter, 30.8 x 21cm

Fire-brick clay, decoration with engobe and oxides,

enamel applied by brush, signed at bottom right

'Chagall', signed and dated on reverse

'Marc Chagall 1951 Vence'

Private collection

39 The Journey Through the Red Sea

(*La traversée de la Mer Rouge*)

1951, platter, 42.5 x 35.5 cm

Moulded and modelled, coloured clay,

decoration with engobe and oxides, glazed,

signed and dated on reverse 'Marc Chagall Vence 1951'

Private collection

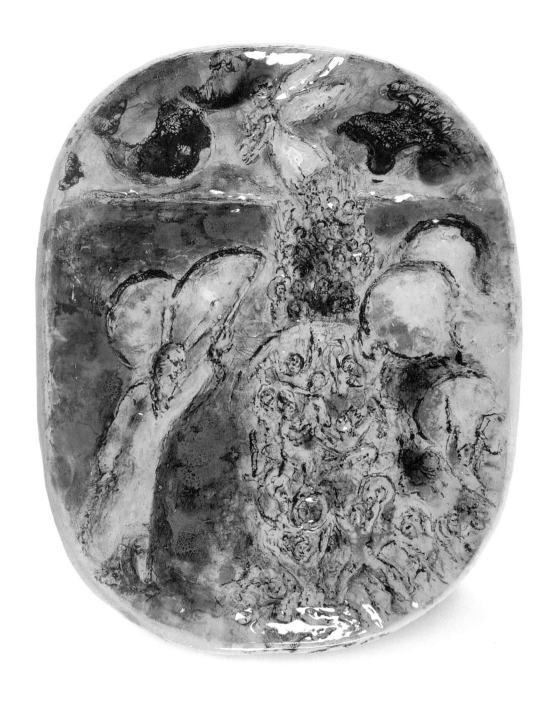

40 Descent from the Cross
(*Descente de croix*)

1951, platter, diameter 30.5 cm

Moulded and modelled, brown clay, decoration with

engobe and oxides, partly with enamel applied

by brush, signed and dated on reverse

'Marc Chagall Vence 1951'

Private collection

41 Descent from the Cross
(*Descente de croix*)

1951, picture platter, 33 x 28.4 cm

Fire-brick clay, decoration with engobe and oxides,

partly with enamel applied by brush,

signed at bottom right 'Chagall', signed and

dated on reverse 'Marc Chagall Vence 1951'

Private collection

42 The Flight to Egypt

(*La fuite en Egypte*)

1951, picture platter, 31 x 31 cm

Fire-brick clay, decoration with engobe and oxides,

partly with enamel applied by brush,

signed and dated on reverse

Private collection

43 Lovers with Basket of Fruit
(*Amoureux au panier de fruits*)

1950–52, plaque (4 tiles), 58 x 60.5 cm

Decorated using oxides on white enamel,

signed bottom left 'Chagall'

Private collection

44 The Clock (*L'horloge*)

1950–52, plaque (12 tiles), 120 x 89 cm

Paint with engobe and oxides on white enamel,

signed twice at bottom right 'Chagall'

Private collection

45 The House (*La maison*)

1952, vase, height 27.5 cm

Turned and modelled, white clay, decoration with
engobe and oxides, incised with knife and etching
needle, glazed, double layer of glaze on inside,
signed on neck 'Chagall'

Private collection, courtesy Yves Lebouc

46 A Summer Night's Dream

(*Le songe d'une nuit d'été*)

1952, vase, height 37.5 cm

Turned, white clay, decoration with engobe

and oxides, incised with knife and etching needle,

partly with enamel applied by brush,

double layer of glaze on inside, signed at bottom,

signed and dated on reverse

Private collection

47 The Woman on the Grey Horse
(*La femme sur le cheval blanc*)
1952, platter, 31 x 35.5 cm
Moulded and modelled, white clay,
decoration with engobe and oxides, incised with knife,
glazed, signed at bottom 'Chagall' and on reverse
'Chagall Vallauris'
Private collection

48 Goat and Cock
(*Chèvre et coq*)
1952, picture platter, 40.6 x 26.5 cm
Fire-brick clay, decoration with engobe and oxides,
enamel applied by brush, signed bottom left 'Chagall'
and on reverse 'Chagall Vallauris'
Private collection

49 David and Bathsheba

(*David et Bethsabée*)

1952, vase, 19.5 x 15.5 cm

Turned and modelled, white clay,

decoration with engobe and oxides, glazed,

double layer of glaze on inside,

signed at bottom 'Chagall' and with dedication

on reverse 'Virginia'

Private collection   Rear view

50 The Red Girl

(*La fille rouge*)

1952, picture platter, 27 x 29.7 cm

Coloured clay, decoration with engobe and oxides,

partly with enamel applied by brush,

signed at bottom right and on reverse 'Chagall'

Private collection

51 The Dream (*Le Songe*)

1952, vase, height 33.5 cm

Moulded, white clay, decoration with engobe

and oxides, incised with knife and etching needle,

partly with enamel applied by brush,

double layer of glaze on inside

Private collection   Rear view

52 The Flying Horse

(*Le cheval s'envole*)

1952, platter, 33 x 25 cm

Moulded, coloured clay, decoration with engobe

and oxides, incised with knife and etching needle,

glazed, signed and dated on reverse

'Marc Chagall 1952'

Private collection

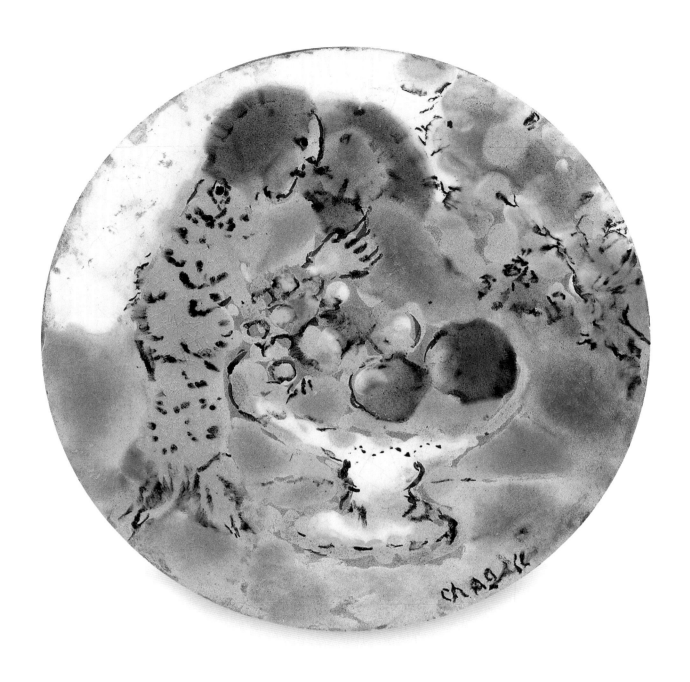

53 Sirens with Fruit

(*Sirènes aux fruits*)

1952, picture platter, diameter 17.2 cm

Coloured clay, decorated using oxides and engobe,

white enamel and glaze partly applied by brush,

signed at bottom right 'Chagall'

Private collection

54 Sculpted Vase

(*Vase sculpté*)

1952, vase, height 45 cm

Turned, hollowed out using a knife, coloured clay,

incised with knife, oxide and enamel applied by brush,

signed at bottom, signed and dated on reverse

Private collection

55 Still Life with Fish

(*Nature morte au poisson*)

1952, tile, 27.7 x 30.2 cm

Coloured clay, decoration with engobe on white engobe,

incised with knife and etching needle,

glazed, signed bottom left 'Chagall',

signed and dated on reverse 'Chagall 1952'

Private collection

56 The Fish (*Le poisson*)

1952, plaque (6 tiles), 58.5 x 87.7 cm

White clay, decorated using oxides on white enamel,

incised with knife and etching needle,

signed at bottom right 'Chagall'

Private collection

57 David and Bathsheba in
the Light of the Moon
(*David et Bethsabée à la lune*)
1952, vase, height 46 cm
Turned, white clay, decoration with engobe and oxides,
partly with enamel applied by brush,
double layer of glaze on inside,
signed and dated on reverse 'Chagall 1952'
Private collection

Rear view

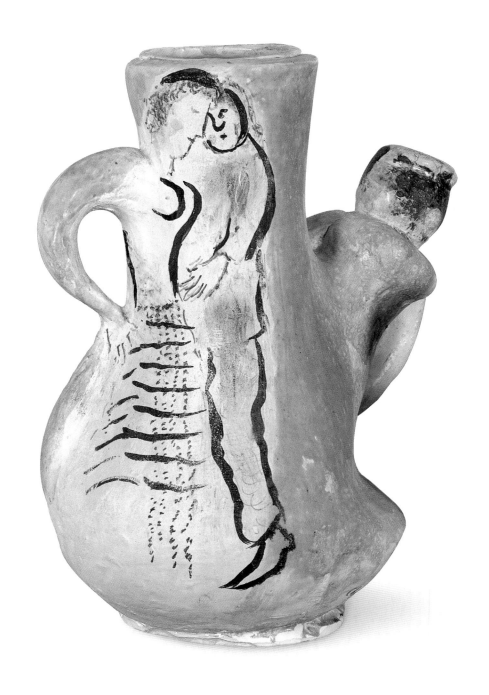

58 Peasant at the Well

(*Le paysan au puits*)

1952/53, vase, height 32 cm

Cast, white clay, decoration with engobe and oxides,

incised using an etching needle,

partly with enamel applied by brush,

signed at base 'Chagall', dated on reverse '1953'

Private collection

59 Peasant at the Well
(*Le paysan au puits*)
1952/53, vase, 33 x 22 cm
Cast, white clay, decoration with engobe and oxides,
incised using an etching needle,
signed at bottom 'Chagall'
Private collection

60 Bird with Crown

(L'oiseau couronné)

1953, platter, diameter 36.5 cm

Moulded, white clay, decoration with engobe and oxides,

incised with knife and etching needle, glazed,

signed and dated on reverse 'Chagall 1953'

Private collection

60 Bird with Crown

61 The Paris Opera (*L'Opéra*)

1953, platter, diameter 33.5 cm

Turned and modelled, fire-brick clay,

decoration with engobe and oxides, glazed,

partly with enamel applied by brush,

signed and dated on reverse 'Marc Chagall 1953'

Private collection

62 The Paris Opera (*L'Opéra*)

1953, platter, 37 x 32.5 cm

Moulded and modelled, white clay,

decoration with engobe and oxides,

partly with enamel applied by brush,

signed and dated on reverse

'1953 Marc Chagall Antibes'

Private collection

63 The Bastille (*La Bastille*)

1953, platter, diameter 31.5 cm

Turned and modelled, decoration with engobe and oxides

Private collection

64 Red Roofs (*Les toits rouges*)

1953, plaque (4 separate tiles), 66 x 60.4 cm

Coloured clay, decoration with engobe and oxides,

incised with knife and etching needle, glazed,

signed at bottom right 'Marc Chagall'

Private collection

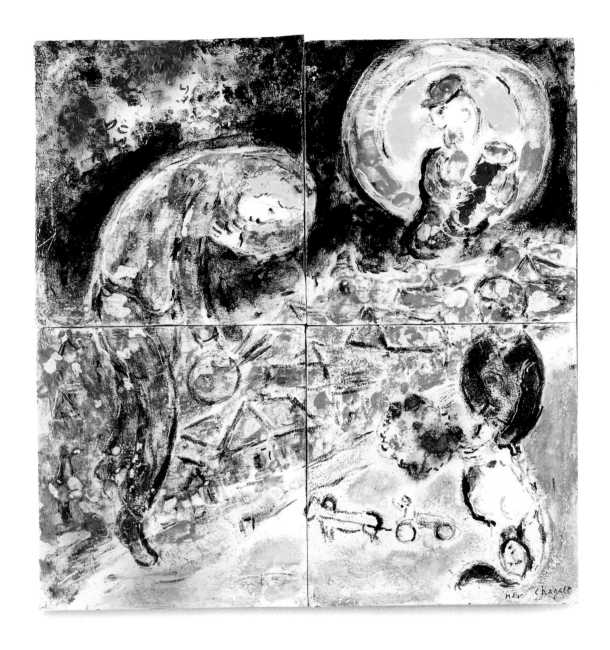

65 In Front of Notre Dame

(*Devant Notre-Dame*)

1953, platter, 42.5 x 31.5 cm

Moulded, decoration with engobe and oxides,

partly with enamel applied by brush,

signed and dated on reverse

Private collection

66 The Offering (*L'offrande*)

1953, platter, diameter 40.5 cm

Moulded, white clay, decoration with engobe and oxides,

signed and dated on reverse

Private collection

67 Nude with Arms Raised
(*Nu aux bras levés*)
1953, platter, diameter 40 cm
Moulded and modelled, coloured clay,
decorated using oxides on white enamel,
signed at bottom right 'Chagall',
signed and dated on reverse
Private collection

68 Two Women (*Deux femmes*)

1953, platter, diameter 40.5 cm

Moulded and modelled, coloured clay,

decorated using oxides on white enamel,

partly with enamel applied by brush,

signed at bottom right 'Chagall',

signed and dated on reverse 'Chagall 1953',

'Madoura' workshop stamp

Private collection

69 Vessel with Hand

(*Vase à la main*)

1953, vase, 15.5 x 20 cm

Turned and modelled, coloured clay,

decorated using oxides on white enamel,

decoration with paraffin, incised with knife,

twice signed and dated on reverse

'Chagall Chagall 1953'

Private collection

70 Woman and Donkey at Night

(*Femme et âne dans la nuit*)

1953, platter, diameter 34.5 cm

Moulded, white clay, decorated using oxides

on black engobe, incised with a knife and etching needle,

glazed, signed and dated on reverse 'Chagall 1953'

Private collection

71 The Chimera (*La chimère*)

1954, vase, height 31 cm

Cast, coloured clay, decoration with white enamel

and oxides, signed at bottom

Private collection

72 The Cock (*Le coq*)

1954, vase, 47 x 41 cm

Cast, coloured clay, decoration with white enamel

and oxides, incised with knife and etching needle,

signed at base 'Marc Chagall'

Private collection

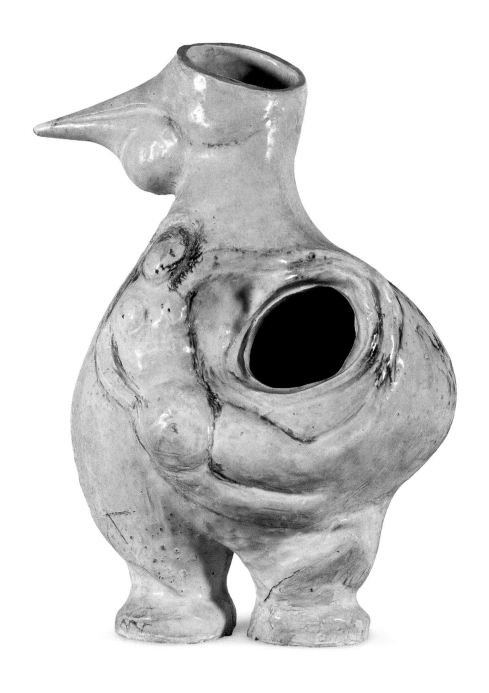

73 The Blue Donkey (*L'âne bleu*)

1954, vase, 31.5 x 22 cm

Cast, decorated using oxides,

incised signature 'Marc Chagall'

Private collection

74 Nude in Profile

(*Nu au profile*)

1954, platter, diameter 25 cm

Moulded, decoration with engobe and oxides,

incised with etching needle, with dedication,

dated and signed on reverse 'Pour Vava 1954 Marc.

Marc Chagall'

Private collection

75 The Journey through the Red Sea

(*La traversée de la Mer Rouge*)

1954, picture platter, 19 x 19 cm

Lava, decoration with enamel and oxides,

signed and dated on reverse

Private collection

76 Pastorale (*Pastorale*)

1955, platter, diameter 25 cm

Turned, decoration with engobe and oxides,

incised with knife

Private collection

77 Figures, Landscape and
Bouquet of Flowers
(*Personnages, paysage et bouquet*)
1955, platter, diameter 24.3 cm
Moulded, decoration with engobe and oxides
on white enamel, incised with knife and etching needle,
glazed, signed at bottom 'Chagall',
signed and dated on reverse 'Chagall 1955'
Private collection

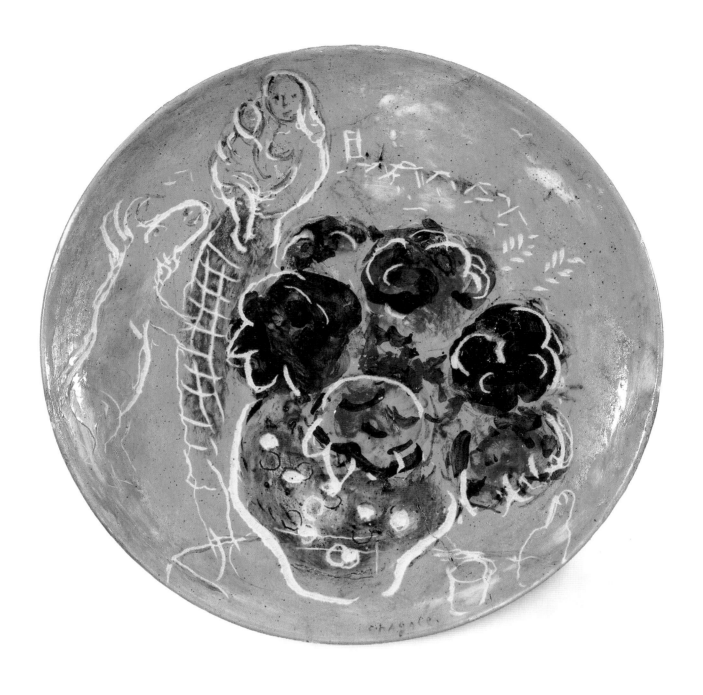

78 Ochre Bouquet (*Bouquet ocre*)

1955, platter, diameter 37 cm

Turned and modelled, fire-brick clay,

decoration with engobe and oxides,

incised with knife and etching needle,

partly with enamel applied by brush,

signed at bottom 'Chagall',

signed and dated on reverse 'Marc Chagall 1955'

Private collection

78 Ochre Bouquet (*Bouquet ocre*)

79 The Lovers and the Beast
(*Les amoureux et la bête*)
1957, vase, height 32 cm
Cast, white clay, decoration with engobe and oxides,
incised with etching needle
Private collection

Rear view

80 The Lovers and the Beast
(*Les amoureux et la bête*)
1957, vase, 32.5 cm
Cast, white clay, decoration with engobe and oxides,
incised with etching needle
Private collection

Rear view

81 The Conversation (*La conversation*)

1958, platter, diameter 32.5 cm

Moulded, signed and dated on reverse

'Chagall Vence 1958'

Private collection

82 Couple with Bouquet of Flowers
in front of St. Paul's
(*Couple au bouquet devant St. Paul*)
1958, platter, diameter 32 cm
Moulded, signed and dated on reverse
'Marc Chagall 1958. Vence'
Private collection

83 Nude against a Blue Background
(*Nu allongé sur fond bleu*)
1958, platter, diameter 40 cm
Plaster, decoration with engobe and oxides,
enamel and glaze, partly applied by brush,
incised with etching needle, worked over by brush,
signed at bottom right 'Chagall', signed and
dated on reverse 'Chagall Marc 1958 Vallauris'
Private collection

84 Nude on Blue Background

(*Nu allongé sur fond bleu*)

1958, diameter 32.5 cm

Plaster, decoration with engobe and oxides,

enamel and glaze, partly applied by brush,

incised with etching needle, worked over by brush,

signed at bottom right 'Chagall', signed and dated

on reverse 'Chagall Marc 1958 Vallauris'

Private collection

85 Couple with Two Fish

(*Couple aux deux poissons*)

1958, platter, 21 x 39 cm

Moulded and modelled, white clay,

decoration with engobe and oxides,

with dedication, signed and dated on reverse

Private collection

86 The Circus (*Cirque*)

1958, platter, 37.5 x 25.2 cm

Moulded, white clay, decoration with engobe and oxides,

incised with knife and etching needle, glazed,

signed and dated on reverse 'Marc Chagall Vence 1958',

'Marius Giuge Vallauris' workshop stamp

Private collection

87 The Creation of Mankind

(*La création de l'homme*)

1959, plaque (2 tiles), 50.4 x 25.1 cm

White clay, decorated using oxides, partly with

enamel applied by brush, signed bottom left 'Chagall'

and at the bottom in the middle 'Marc Chagall'

Private collection

88 The Creation of Mankind
(*La création de l'homme*)
1959, plaque (2 tiles), 50.4 x 25.1 cm
White clay, decorated using oxides,
partly with enamel applied by brush,
signed at bottom right 'Chagall'
Private collection

89 The Stroll (*La promenade*)

1961, vase, height 26 cm

Moulded, brown clay, decoration with engobe

and oxides, partly with enamel applied by brush,

incised with knife and etching needle,

signed and dated on reverse 'Chagall Vallauris 1961'

Private collection

90 The Two Birds (*Les deux oiseaux*)

1961, platter, 26 x 43 cm

Moulded and modelled, white clay,

decoration with engobe and oxides,

incised with knife and etching needle,

glaze and enamel partly applied by brush,

signed at bottom 'Chagall', signed and dated

on reverse 'Chagall Vallauris 1961'

Private collection

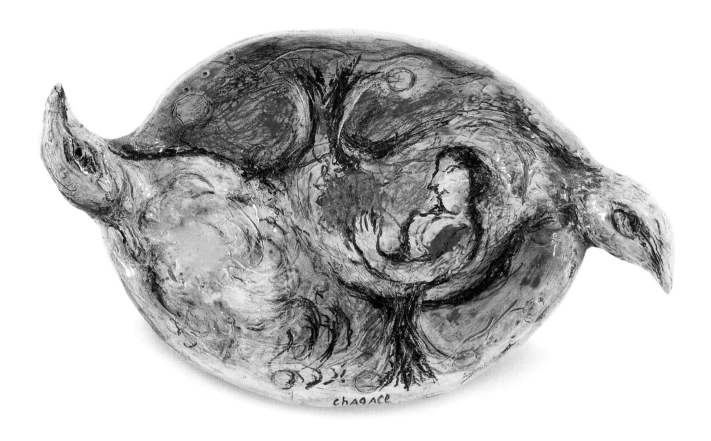

91 Greek Landscape (*Paysage de Grèce*)

1962, plaque (6 tiles), 50 x 75 cm

White clay, decorated using oxides on white enamel,

signed and dated at bottom right '1962 Marc Chagall'

Private collection

92 The Couple (*Le couple*)

1962, platter, 64 x 34 cm

Moulded and modelled, decoration with white enamel,

engobe and oxides, incised with knife and etching needle,

signature incised at bottom 'Chagall',

signed on reverse 'Chagall Marc'

Private collection

93 Large Figures (*Grands personnages*)

1962, vase, height 45 cm

Turned and modelled, white clay, decorated using oxides,

incised with knife and etching needle, glazed,

double layer of glaze inside

Private collection

Rear view

94 Couple with Bouquet of Flowers

(*Couple au bouquet*)

1962, platter, 32 x 27.5 cm

Private collection

95 Mauve Vase (*Vase mauve*)

1962, vase, height 43 cm

Turned, white clay, decoration with engobe and oxides,

incised with knife and etching needle, partly with enamel

applied by brush, double layer of glaze inside,

signed on reverse

Private collection

96 Woman with Flowers
(*Femme et fleurs*)

1962, vase, height 41 cm

Turned and modelled, white clay, decoration with

engobe and oxides, incised with knife, white enamel,

partly applied by brush, double layer of glaze inside,

signed and dated at bottom 'Marc Chagall 1962'

'Het Kruithuis' Ceramics Museum, s'Hertogenbosch,

Netherlands

Selected Bibliography

Alexander, Sidney, *Marc Chagall. A Biography*,
New York 1989

Berger, Roland/Dietmar Winkler, *Zirkusbilder*,
Altenburg 1983

Bohm-Duchen, Monica, *Chagall*, London 1998

Cassou, Jean, *Chagall*, Paris 1982

Chagall, Marc, *Ma vie*, Paris 1995

Compton, Susan, *Marc Chagall. My Life – My Dream.
Berlin and Paris 1922–1940*, Munich 1990

Crespelle, Jean-Paul, *Chagall, L'amour, le rêve et
la vie*, Paris 1969

Doschka, Roland (ed.), *Marc Chagall. Origins and
Paths*, Munich/New York 1998

Forestier, Sylvie/Meret Meyer, *Chagall y la ceramica*,
Milan 1990

German, Michail, *Marc Chagall. Le pays qui se trouve
en mon âme: la Russie*, Bornemouth 1995

Güse, Ernst-Gerhard (ed.), *Marc Chagall. Druckgraphik*,
Stuttgart 1994

Haftmann, Werner, *Marc Chagall: Gouachen, Zeichnungen,
Aquarelle*, Cologne 1975

Kamenski, Alexander, *Chagall, période russe et
soviétique 1907–1922* Paris 1988

Kuthy, Sandor/Meret Meyer, *Marc Chagall 1907–1917*,
Bern 1996

Le Target, François, *Marc Chagall*, Barcelona 1985

Longus, *Daphnis and Chloe*, with lithographs by
Marc Chagall, Munich 1994

Makarius, Michel, *Chagall*, Paris 1987

Malraux, André/Charles Sorlier, *Les Céramiques
et Sculptures de Chagall*, Monaco 1972

Marchesseau, Daniel, *Chagall, ivre d'images*, Paris 1995

Meyer, Franz, *Marc Chagall, Leben und Werk*,
Cologne 1961

Meyer, Franz, *Marc Chagall*, Paris 1995

Schmalenbach, Walter/Charles Sorlier, *Marc Chagall*,
Paris/Frankfurt 1979

Schneider, Pierre, *Chagall à travers le siècle*, Paris 1995

Sorlier, Charles, *Marc Chagall et Ambroise Vollard*,
Paris 1981

Souverbie, Marie-Thérèse, *Chagall*, New York 1975

Venturi, Lionello, *Chagall*, Paris 1966

Vitali, Christoph (ed.), *Marc Chagall. Die Russischen
Jahre 1906–1922*, Bern 1991

Walther, Ingo F./Rainer Metzger, *Marc Chagall
1887–1985. Malerei als Poesie*, Cologne 1993

Werner, Alfred, *Chagall Watercolors and Gouaches*,
New York 1970 (1977)

Photographic Credits

All photographs of the works by Marc Chagall come
from Ewald Graber, Bern – Archives Marc Chagall, Paris,
with the exception of the following:

pp. 14, 15, 18, 23: Archives Marc Chagall, Paris

pp. 68, 94–95: Fabrice Gousset

p. 16: IZIS

pp. 11, 12, 17: Jaca Book, Milan

pp. 33, 173 (spine and p. 25 (detail), p. 1):
Courtesy Yves Lebouc

p. 170: Courtesy Malingue

p. 21: RA-Gamma Liaison/Frank Spooner Picture, London

Frontispiece and pp. 65, 13: Studio Fink, Hildrizhausen

p. 22: Studio Maeght

p. 18: André Villers

12.50